Why do people invent things?

Inventors try to solve problems. They think about people's needs, and then try to come up with an answer. When an inventor noticed how inconvenient big umbrellas were, he invented a folding one that would fit into a bag.

Gone to buy some glue!

Post-it notes were invented by accident when someone made a glue that didn't stick properly. You could stick down a piece of paper, peel it off, and then restick it!

Some inventions are just for fun. The first Frisbees were empty pie tins belonging to a baker called Joseph Frisbie. When some of his customers tossed the tins to each other in the park, the idea for the Frisbee was born.

Zippers Have Teeth

and other questions
about inventions

Barbara Taylor

KINGFISHER

NEW YORK

Copyright © Kingfisher 2012
Published in the United States by Kingfisher,
175 Fifth Ave., New York, NY 10010
Kingfisher is an imprint of Macmillan Children's Books,
London.
All rights reserved.

First published 1996 by Kingfisher

Distributed in the U.S. and Canada by Macmillan, 175 Fifth
Ave., New York, NY 10010

Library of Congress Cataloging-in-Publication data has been
applied for.

ISBN: 978-0-7534-6801-2

Kingfisher books are available for special promotions and
premiums. For details contact: Special Markets Department,
Macmillan, 175 Fifth Ave., New York, NY 10010.

For more information, please visit www.kingfisherbooks.com

Printed in China
9 8 7 6 5 4 3 2 1

1TR/0612/UTD/WKT/140MA

Illustrations: Susanna Addario 28-29; Mike Bergin cover; Mike
Davis 7t; Peter Dennis (Linda Rogers) 10-11, 18-19; Chris
Forsey, 22tl, 26tl, 30-31; Terry Gabbey (AFA Ltd.) 20-21; Ruby
Green 14-15, 26-27; Nick Harris (Virgil Pomfret) 24-25; Biz
Hull (Artist Partners) 16-17; Tony Kenyon (BL Kearley) all
cartoons; Nicki Palin 6-7, 8-9, 12-13; Roger Stuart 4-5, 22-23

Please note: because of the young reading level of this
book, trademarked names only carry a trademark symbol
in the index.

Credit: JPL/NASA 31t

CONTENTS

Safety pins were introduced more than 150 years ago, but have a much longer history. Their inventor copied the idea from clasps worn by the ancient Egyptians.

Is everything invented?

No it isn't! An invention is something new like a paper clip, which didn't exist before someone thought of it. But things like coal and rubber weren't invented. They were already in the world, and just had to be discovered.

When people first discovered the milky juice of the rubber tree they used it to make rubber. Later, someone invented rubber tires for cars and bicycles.

Where do inventors get their ideas?

Inventors get ideas for their inventions in many different places. Some of them study plants and animals to see how they have solved their problems. Others look at ideas from other places or from the past. Very few ideas come out of nowhere.

Burdock seeds are covered with tiny hooks that stick to things, but can be pulled off. An engineer who noticed this used his discovery to make Velcro for fastenings.

Which new invention was soon on everybody's lips?

In 1915 American scientists came up with a small invention that was a huge success. It was a creamy, color crayon inside a case that could be wound up and used in a second—the very first lipstick.

Ancient Egyptian women didn't have wind-up lipsticks, but they did color their lips. They used golden clay mixed with juicy tree sap.

Who wore a mouthful of hippo teeth?

About 2,500 years ago people began to make false teeth from ivory or bone. Hippo bone was popular, but so were ox, cat, and human bones. Unfortunately, all these false teeth soon turned brown and started to rot. Yuck!

Before lipsticks, lip colors came in a pot. Many of them were waxes and ointments colored with plant dyes such as grape juice.

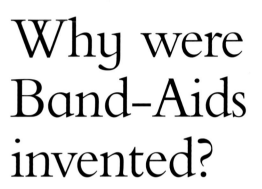

The very first hair dryers were made from vacuum cleaners! Alexandre Godefoy invented the first electric hair dryer in 1890.

Why were Band-Aids invented?

Earle Dickson invented Band-Aids for his wife, who kept cutting herself in the kitchen. He stuck small squares of cloth on to pieces of tape, covering them carefully to stop the glue drying out. Whenever his wife cut herself, she grabbed a piece of the tape, and stuck it on.

Before Mr. King Camp Gillette invented safe, modern razors in 1895, men shaved with sharp cutthroat razors—and hoped that their hand wouldn't slip!

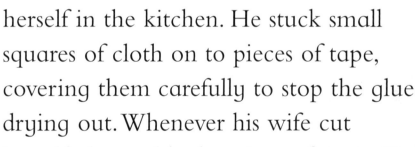

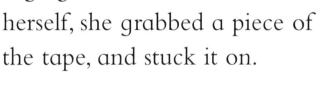

Who first flushed the toilet?

Four hundred years ago Sir John Harrington built a flushing toilet for his godmother, Queen Elizabeth I. In those days very few homes had water pipes or drains, so ordinary people had to carry on using their chamber pots.

The problem with this shower from the 1800s was that you had to pump the water yourself— by foot. No wonder it never really caught on!

About 100 years ago, flush toilets were highly-prized pieces of furniture. They were often beautifully decorated with fruit, flowers, animals, or shells.

Who first jumped in the bath?

The people of Greece, Rome, and the Indus Valley in Pakistan all enjoyed a bath in ancient times. But, as time went by, baths went out of fashion and many people never even washed. They used perfumes to cover up the stink!

The Chinese used pigs' hairs to make the first toothbrushes more than 500 years ago. Luckily for pigs, nylon brushes came along in the 1930s!

How did horses help keep carpets clean?

The first carpet-cleaning machine was towed by horses! It was parked outside the house because of its smelly gasoline engine. Long pipes stretched through the windows and sucked up all of the dirt. It was a spectacle and people often invited their friends around to watch!

Who invented raincoats?

A lot of today's rainwear is made from PVC. It's a plastic-backed material which comes in lots of bright colours.

The first waterproof raincoats were made in 1823 by Charles Macintosh. He made the cloth waterproof by sandwiching a layer of rubber between two lengths of cotton. The coats kept people dry, but they were very heavy and smelled awful when they were wet!

It rains so much in Scotland that hill farmers buy raincoats for their sheep!

Why do zippers have teeth?

Without their teeth, zippers couldn't open or close. The two rows of teeth are joined by a slider, which locks them together or pulls them apart. Zippers were invented in the 1890s, and were a great improvement on fiddly buttons and hooks and eyes.

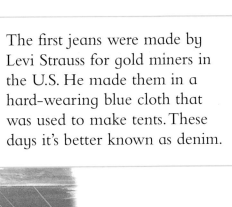

The first jeans were made by Levi Strauss for gold miners in the U.S. He made them in a hard-wearing blue cloth that was used to make tents. These days it's better known as denim.

Can clothes keep you feeling fit?

Some clothing can help keep you healthy. Support tights can improve blood flow and help prevent blood clots and other circulation problems.

When Thomas Hancock invented elastic in 1820, he thought it would be useful along the tops of pockets to stop thieves. It was someone else who realized it would be perfect for holding up people's underwear!

What did people use before refrigerators?

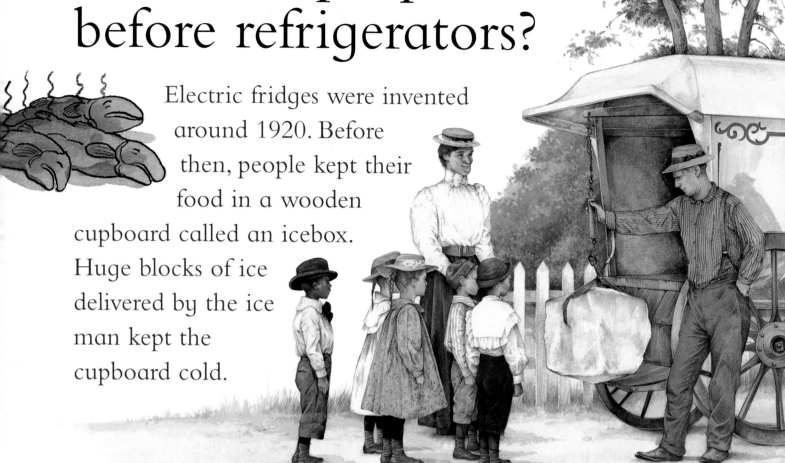

Electric fridges were invented around 1920. Before then, people kept their food in a wooden cupboard called an icebox. Huge blocks of ice delivered by the ice man kept the cupboard cold.

Coca-Cola didn't start out as a soda pop. An American chemist named John Pemberton invented it as a sweet syrup in 1885. Soda water was added to it later.

Who ate the first cornflakes?

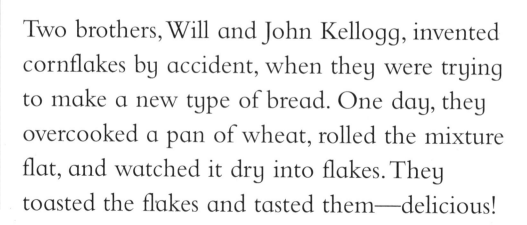

Two brothers, Will and John Kellogg, invented cornflakes by accident, when they were trying to make a new type of bread. One day, they overcooked a pan of wheat, rolled the mixture flat, and watched it dry into flakes. They toasted the flakes and tasted them—delicious!

The ice man called several times a week to deliver large blocks of ice for the icebox.

Long ago, people made natural fridges by lining caves and holes with a thick layer of snow in winter. These ice houses kept fresh food cool all the way through the warm summer months.

In 1853, a new food was invented. When a diner asked for extrathin fries, the chef came up with the first potato chips.

How were drinking straws invented?

One hot summer in the 1880s, a man named Marvin Stone made the first paper straw. He had noticed that people kept drinks cooler by not touching the glass and using a hollow grass stalk to suck up the liquid.

Why are bears called teddy bears?

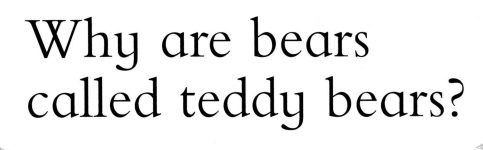

Teddy bears are named after the American president, Theodore Roosevelt, who was called Teddy for short. Once, on a hunting trip, he came across a bear cub and refused to shoot it. A candy store owner who read about the story in the paper decided to give up his store and make toy bears. He called them teddy bears, after the president.

The construction toys Meccano and Lego were both invented to encourage children to build things—not destroy them! You can use them to make all kinds of inventions!

The Chinese probably invented playing cards over 1,000 years ago.

SNAP!

Which toy is 6,000 years old?

Dolls are probably the oldest toys of all. Roman children played with dolls made of rags. Dolls have been made from all sorts of materials—wood, wax, paper, china, and plastic.

Barbie first went on sale in 1959. She was the first-ever doll to have a grown-up's body.

When did home computer games appear?

The first home computer games appeared in 1974. Compared to today's games, they weren't very exciting. There were no life-and-death battles in outer space—you hit a ball back and forth with a bat!

How do you make toast without a toaster?

People made toast long before there were electric toasters. They put a piece of bread on the end of a long toasting fork, and held it in front of a fire. Unfortunately, the bread burned easily, and needed very careful watching. The first pop-up toaster was invented in the U.S. more than 85 years ago.

Electric toasters save us from having to keep an eye on the toast—and from burning it, too!

In 1937 an automatic tea-making machine was invented. It heated water, made the tea, and then woke you with an alarm. At first it was called the Cheerywake, but it was soon renamed the Teasmade.

Who invented the microwave oven?

Microwaves are invisible waves of energy. When they're beamed at food, any water in the food starts to shake violently, and gets very hot. The heat passes quickly through the food, and cooks it all the way through.

Percy Spencer invented the microwave oven just after World War II. He had been working on ways of using invisible waves to detect enemy planes. When the waves melted the candy bar in his pocket, he realized they would be useful for cooking, too!

About 100 years ago, only rich people had electricity in their homes. The first electrical gadgets were dangerous things, and servants sometimes risked their lives by using them.

Why don't nonstick frying pans stick?

Nonstick pans don't stick because they are coated with something as slippery as ice, called Teflon. Teflon is actually a kind of plastic, and was invented in the late 1930s. But it took years for someone to come up with the idea of sticking the stuff onto a frying pan!

17

Who scored goals in a basket?

The very first basketball players used two old peach baskets as goals. Basketball was invented in 1891 by coach James Naismith, who was looking for an exciting game to play indoors on cold winter nights.

Why are sneakers so springy?

Sneakers have springy soles made of rubber and little pockets of air. Each time you take a step, the rubber gets squashed down, but quickly springs back to its original size. All this squashing and springing makes your feet bounce off the ground, and helps you to run a little faster.

Early basketball players had to climb a ladder to get the ball back after a goal. Things are easier today—now the goal nets have a hole in the bottom.

Roller-skating was all the rage in the late 1800s. At the ballet in Paris, ballerinas even danced in them!

How did people ice-skate in summer?

Before there were ice rinks, people could only ice-skate outdoors in the winter. Then someone came up with the idea of making a "ground" skate that people could enjoy in the summer, too. Instead of a blade, they put wheels on the sole and suddenly—the roller skate had arrived!

Jet Skis first went on sale in Japan in 1979. Jet Skiers have to steer clear of bathers. The very latest models can zoom along at speeds of more than 80 mph (130 km/h).

What were the first cars like?

The first cars were steam engines on wheels—noisy, smoky machines that scared other road users! But these steam cars soon got quicker and easier to drive. They were used for almost 30 years, until they were replaced by faster cars with gasoline engines.

In the 1930s, planes carried 20 passengers at the most. By the 1970s, the new jumbo jets could seat up to 500. Today, superjumbos can carry as many as 850 people!

How do you ride on air?

People ride on air every time they travel on a hovercraft. The hovercraft was invented by Christopher Cockerell in 1959. He discovered that trapping a cushion of air beneath a boat lifts it up above the waves, allowing it to travel much faster.

The penny-farthing bicycle was invented in the 1860s. It had two wheels—one very large and one very small—and was named after two British coins of the time—the large penny and the tiny farthing.

Everybody knows about seat belts for people to wear, but did you know that cats and dogs can wear them too? So strap in, Felix!

The first cars weren't allowed to go faster than 1.9 mph (3km/h). And someone had to walk in front with a flag to warn other road users!

Which bikes have sails?

The fastest superbikes have solid wheels and flat frames that work in the same way as a sail. As the bike zooms along, its wheels and frame catch the wind, which helps push the bike forward—exactly as it does on a boat. But most of the power still comes from turning the pedals!

How can you fit 1,500 books in your pocket?

There is room to store about 1,500 books on an eBook reader— a small, slimline electronic device that is designed to hold and display a digital library of books. It is about the size of a novel and can easily be slipped into a coat pocket.

The Egyptians were one of the first peoples to write with ink. They made it by mixing black soot with sticky tree sap.

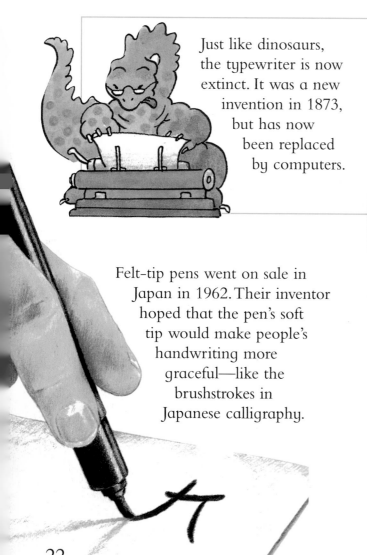

Just like dinosaurs, the typewriter is now extinct. It was a new invention in 1873, but has now been replaced by computers.

Felt-tip pens went on sale in Japan in 1962. Their inventor hoped that the pen's soft tip would make people's handwriting more graceful—like the brushstrokes in Japanese calligraphy.

Which computer was as big as a bus?

Today's pocket calculators can carry out calculations much quicker than you can move your fingers. They are as powerful as the huge computers of the 1960s.

The first computer was about as long as four buses and was called Colossus. It was built in Britain and was switched on in 1943. Few people knew about it at the time, because one of its first jobs was to crack secret codes in World War II.

Who was Mr. Biro?

László Bíró invented the ballpoint pen in 1938. It contained a tube of long-lasting, quick-drying ink, which rolled evenly onto the paper thanks to a tiny ball at the tip. In the U.K. most people now call their ballpoint a biro!

How did a till settle a row?

In James Ritty's saloon in Ohio, the customers were always arguing with the staff about how much they had to pay for their drinks. So in 1879 Ritty invented a cash register, which rang up the prices, kept a record of how much money was in the till, and gave Ritty and his staff a more peaceful life.

Since 1980, goods sold in stores have had a bar code on them. Only a laser scanner can understand the bar code's pattern, which contains all kinds of information about the item.

Who used tea as money?

People in Tibet and China once used tea pressed into blocks as money. Before coins were invented, people used to swap things like shells, beads, or grain for the goods they wanted.

The Chinese first used paper banknotes about 1,200 years ago. They printed some of their notes on the bark of the mulberry tree.

How can a shopping cart make you rich?

Inventions don't have to be grand. When Margaret Knight invented flat-bottomed paper bags, she became a wealthy woman. The bags held twice as much shopping as an ordinary bag!

The person who invented the world's first shopping cart became a millionaire. Sylvan Goldman's cart was little more than a chair on wheels, with two baskets fitted on the top, but it earned him a fortune.

Which came first— screws or screwdrivers?

Spiral or twisted nails were used in the 1500s in guns, armor, and clocks. But, strangely, you couldn't unscrew a screw for another 300 years, when the handy screwdriver first appeared.

Today's carpenters use many of the same tools as carpenters used long ago.

Screws weren't made by machine until the 1760s. The thread that runs around the screw had to be filed by hand. That must have been a fiddly task!

Who had everything under lock and key?

The ancient Egyptians invented locks. Two wooden bolts fitted together snugly and were held in place by pins arranged in a pattern. The pins could only be freed with a key which had a matching pattern.

With grow bags you can grow plants anywhere—even if you don't have a garden. These big bags of earth first appeared in 1973.

Could a horse mow the lawn?

The first lawnmowers were pulled by horses. The animals had to wear big rubber boots so they didn't leave messy hoof prints all over the freshly-mown lawn!

Lawnmower engines were used on the first go-karts. Today people adapt all sorts of different engines, from chainsaw to car engines, to power their karts.

Who took hours to take a photo?

In the late 1800s, it took so long to take a photo that sitters needed a back-rest to help them sit still!

A Frenchman called Joseph Niépce took the first-ever photograph in 1826. He had to wait eight hours before the picture was captured on a thin metal plate coated with a sort of tar. The photo was of the view from his window.

Niépce would have found it hard to believe that today's digital cameras can take hundreds of pictures in just minutes, which can then be viewed and stored on the camera itself!

When could you watch pink TV?

The first TV had an odd picture— bright pink and very fuzzy! But its inventor, John Logie Baird, had used very odd equipment to build it—including a bicycle light and a knitting needle!

The world's smallest radio is about the size of a pea!

Who invented the personal stereo?

The Walkman was the very first personal stereo. It was invented in 1979 by a Japanese electrical company called Sony, and was a small portable cassette player with headphones.

The first telephone service started in 1878, in a small town in the U.S. Only 20 people had phones, so they could only call each other!

How can you fight a hungry dinosaur?

As you press buttons in the special data glove, the computer changes the pictures you see and the sounds you hear.

When you put on a virtual reality helmet, you enter an imaginary world. You could be fighting a man-eating dinosaur or visiting aliens in space. Everything inside the helmet looks and sounds real, but is actually created by a computer.

Anyone can be an inventor! What would you like to invent?

Scientists are experimenting with fruit and vegetables to produce useful, tasty foods. One day they may come up with square tomatoes which you can stack neatly on a shelf.

Are there robots in space?

Scientists have developed many robots to study and explore the planets, and to help astronauts working in space. Some of the most advanced are the rover robots, built to search for life and water on Mars. Equipped with a drill and scientific equipment to take and analyze rock samples, these robots can even select their own route from one location on the planet's surface to the next.

Many cars today are fitted with a GPS Navigator—a satellite navigation system which allows drivers to plan their routes and avoid traffic.

Index